NONE
DARE
CALL
IT
TREASON!

BOOK 15

The House That Hiss Built
The Anti American United Nations!

Robert W. Pelton
$4.95

1

"*Treason doth never prosper,*

    "*What's the reason?*

"*Why if it prosper,*

    "*None dare call it treason.*"

    John Harrington

Printed in America
On Recycled Paper
In
Charleston, South Carolina

Published in America
By
The Freedom & Liberty
Foundation Press
Knoxville, Tennessee

Dedicated
To

The greatest, most generous, most benevolent and most powerful nation on the face of the earth – and the only country in the history of the world to have been founded on Biblical principles.

A nation can survive its fools, and even the ambitious. But it cannot survive treason from within.

An enemy at the gates is less formidable, for he is known and he carries his banners openly.

The traitor moves among those within the gates freely, his sly whispers rustling through the galleys, heard in the very hall of government itself.

For the traitor appears not traitor. He speaks in the accent familiar to his victims, and he wears their face and their garments, and he appeals to the baseness that lies deep in the hearts of all men.

He rots the soul of a nation - he works secretly and unknown in the night to undermine the pillars of a city - he infects the body politic so that it can no longer resist.

A murderer is less to be feared.

Cicero, 42 B.C.

CONTENTS

Forward

Independence Hall Where the Declaration of Independence Was Signed.

Our glorious Declaration of Independence is a timeless divinely inspired masterpiece given to mankind through the anointed pen of Thomas Jefferson.
The grand and unmatched United States Constitution is indisputably the product of Providential guidance and wisdom

and certainly not a document which evokes whimsical interpretations with the changing political climates.

All Americans have a moral obligation to stand up and be counted in these trying times!

Abraham Lincoln boldly declared: *"To sin by silence when they should protest, makes cowards of men."*

William Lloyd Garrison capsulized it best: *"As a free man who is determined to remain free -- I do not wish to think or speak, or write with moderation. "Tell a man whose house is on fire to give a moderate alarm; tell him to moderately rescue his wife from the hands of a ravisher; tell the mother to gradually extricate her babe from the fire into which it has fallen -- but urge me not to use moderation in a course like the present."*

Senator Barry Goldwater, 1964 Presidential candidate was castigated and verbally crucified by the media.

He simply stated this simple truism: *"Extremism in the pursuit of Liberty is no vice."*

This good and moral man of character soundly rocked the boat of the propagandists. He was as a result soundly defeated in the election.

The alarmed media wolves panicked the voters with their jeers and sneers and insane howls about this man's lack of *"moderation!"*

It can honestly be said that through the Providential genius of our Founding Fathers, the remaining remnants of the original American Constitutional Republic still provides more freedom, opportunity and abundance for mankind than is found in any other nation in the world.

This is true despite decade after decade of unabated treason and treachery promulgated by innumerable traitorous individuals found buried in the twiddle dee – twiddle dum administrations of both the Democrats and the Republicans.

An informed and active, not a media brainwashed electorate, is the only antidote to further prostitution of, and the ultimate destruction of, what Benjamin Franklin called our Republic.

Preface

"Treason against the United States shall consist only in levying war against them, or in adhering to their enemies, giving them aid and comfort."

U.S. Constitution. Article 111, Section 3

What is your treason I.Q.?

If you can answer the following questions, it's high.

If you miss one or more, you should read the *None Dare Call It Treason* series!

Who was behind allowing Red Chinese soldiers take airborne training at Fort Benning, Georgia?

Is this not treason?

Why was South Vietnam, South Africa, Rhodesia and numerous other American friends deliberately betrayed to the forces of evil?

Is this not treason?

Why was our friend Chiang Kai Shek not so gently coerced into a Communist dictatorship by highly placed subversives in the State Department?

Is this not treason?

Why was Cuba treasonously delivered into the clutches of Communist revolutionary Fidel Castro?

Is this not treason?

Why have untold millions of dollars consistently been used to prop up faltering Red dictatorships and to assist Communist terrorists in overthrowing non-Communist governments?

Is this not treason?

What American company sold nuclear reactors to Communist Occupied Romania?

Is this not treason?

Name the company that provided Communist Hungary with a factory designed to make 1.5 million light bulbs daily?

Is this not treason?

What well known oil company invested $1 billion for oil exploration in Communist Occupied Angola?

Is this not treason?

Can you name the American company who treasonously built and equipped a $10 million electronics plant near Warsaw for the Polish slave labor tyranny?

Is this not treason?

These are questions to which every American should rightfully have an honest answer.

Unfortunately most do not!

Tragedy was carefully orchestrated by traitors in our Government and the media with regard to Cuba, Vietnam, Laos, Cambodia, Rhodesia, China, El Salvador, Nicaragua and many other countries.

Anastasio Somoza was the former President of free Nicaragua.

He offered this startling insight in his 1980 book, Nicaragua Betrayed: *"I have factual evidence that the betrayal of Nicaragua was not perpetrated out of ignorance, but rather by design."*

Somoza was soon after assassinated!

Is this not treason?

John Lehman, Secretary of the Navy, made this shocking statement on May 25 to the 1983 Annapolis graduating class: *"Within weeks many of you will be looking across just hundreds of feet of water at some of the most modern technology ever invented in America.*

"Unfortunately, it is on Soviet ships."

Is this not treason?

Earl E.T. Smith was the American Ambassador to Cuba when it was similarly delivered to the Communists.

He makes this concise comment on July 14, 1986: *"Nicaragua is Cuba all over again."*

Can you name the company that paid the Communist dictatorship in Angola over $600 million annually in taxes and oil royalties.

This money bought new Soviet jets, tanks and helicopter gunships.

And it paid Castro for supplying 35,000 imported Cuban mercenaries who keep the Angolan people enslaved.

Is this not treason?

Stressed retired Brigadier General Andrew J. Gatsis on August 11, 1986: *"Though aware of the Communist goal of world domination, the average U.S. Citizen refuses to believe that the real threat comes from governmental officials and their non-governmental confederates who secretly espouse the same objectives as the openly avowed Communists."*

Anthony Sutton stated in his 1986 book *The Best Enemy Money Can Buy: "We now have the formidable task of bringing these gentlemen to the bar of justice to publicly answer for their private and concealed actions."*

The *None Dare Call It Treason* series certainly won't win accolades from the United Nations or the State Department!

Nor will Harvard feel compelled to bestow an honorary degree upon the author!

Harvard Law School was the spawning ground for an incredible number of Red agents. Included were members of the first Soviet spy ring ever to be exposed in our government.

Reed Irvine aptly commented in July of 1986: *"Indeed, it has long been a joke among refugees from Eastern Europe that there are more Marxists at Harvard than there are in the Soviet Union, or Poland, or whatever Communist country the refugee called home."*

The Honorable Ezra Taft Benson said:

 *"The truth must be told even at the risk of destroying, in large measure, the influence of men who are widely respected and loved by the American people.*

"The stakes are high. Freedom and survival is the issue."

Treason is still a most serious federal offense.

The *None Dare Call It Treason* series examines the reasons for and the Americans behind the fall of freedom and the rise of tyranny throughout the world!

Has anything really changed?
You Decide!

Treason

Whoever, owing allegiance to the United States, levies war against them or adheres to their enemies, giving them aid and comfort within the United States or elsewhere, is guilty of treason and shall suffer death, or be imprisoned not less than five years and fined not less than $10,000; and shall be incapable of holding any office under the United states.

U.S. Code, Title 18, Section 2381

Whoever, owing allegiance to the United States and having knowledge of the commission of any treason against them, conceals and does not, as soon as may be, disclose and make known the same to the President or to some judge of the United States, or to the Governor or to some judge or justice of a particular state, is guilty of misprision of treason, and shall be fined not more than $1000 or imprisoned not more than 7 years or both.

U.S. Code, Title 18, Section 2382

The House That Hiss Built
The
Anti-American
United Nations!

Treason: *"The betrayal of one's country, esp. by giving aid to an enemy."*

The American Heritage Dictionary

Equality of membership in the United Nations with such primitive societies is an absurdity of such ludicrous proportions as to make the anatomy of a giraffe seem reasonable.

A Sordid Tale

of

Deceit

&

Treason

in

America

New York City is the home of two well known houses. The one in the Bronx -- Yankee Stadium -- is called *"The House that Ruth Built."*
It's American as Mom, the flag and apple pie!
The other in Manhattan -- the United Nations -- is called *"The House that Hiss Built."*

It's as Communist occupied as is Moscow, Minsk or Riga!

The United Nations headquarters could hardly be in a better place from the standpoint of America's implacable Red enemies and their spying activities.

The glass enclosed stable for the Trojan Horse on the East River is a monumental welfare agency for Communist slave labor dictatorships throughout the world!

Nor could it be in a worse place from the standpoint of America's national security!

For example, FBI Director J. Edgar Hoover said this: *"They are guests of the United States and are supposedly dedicated in the cause if international peace.*

"But they are in fact carefully selected envoys of the international Communist conspiracy, trained in trickery and deceit and dedicated to the concept of fully exploiting the freedoms of the countries they seek to destroy.

Punishment for espionage activities, while an employee of the UN is nonexistent!

Any Communist caught spying is simply sent back home and replaced by another spy!

Columnist Henry J. Taylor offered this: *"865 Soviet-bloc personnel and more than 1,200 dependents all with diplomatic immunity against arrest, and more of them accredited to the United Nations are stationed here.*

"About 80 percent of the Soviet-bloc personnel are intelligence officers and not diplomats at all. Nothing could be a heavier blow to Red espionage than to put the UN headquarters elsewhere."

Chiao Kuan-hua was one of Communist Occupied China's most important spies.

He headed Peking's first UN delegation!

U.S. intelligence calls Huang Hua who was Chiao's top aide *"a gifted saboteur and espionage artist."*

Said columnist Paul Scott: *"Espionage will be an even greater danger now that Red China has been admitted to the UN.*

"Since the size of each country's UN delegation and staff reflects the size of the country's population, and since Red China has between 700 and 800 million people, she might be allowed 3,000 or more diplomats and staff members, each of whom would possess diplomatic immunity.

"The most obvious and practical solution to the drug and spying dangers to our country is to get the U.S. out of the United Nations and the UN out of the United States."

The United Nations is no more than a Marxist-Leninist propaganda machine!

It's a subversive international organization conceived by Communists, designed by Communists, staffed by Communists and permanently under the control of Communists!

It was all planned that way from the very beginning!

Arkady N. Shevchenko defected to the United States in April, 1978.

This Russian was Undersecretary for Political and Security Council Affairs at the UN.

He charged: *"Soviet intelligence officers have become a Trojan horse behind the wall of the United Nations.*

"New York City is the most important base of all Soviet intelligence operations in the world!"

"There has never been any doubt about the United Nations importance as a global beehive of Soviet agents" suggested Hilaire duBerrier.

The UN was headquartered in the United States because Communist Occupied Russia insisted it be placed on American soil!

It operates solely to further the objectives and to achieve the goals of Communists and Communism!

The public record speaks for itself!

Communist espionage agent Alger Hiss was the darling of Roosevelt's and the Washington *"liberals."*

He moved with ease from Agriculture to Justice to State.

Radical leftist Dean Acheson was the Assistant Secretary of State under Stettinius.

On May 1, 1944 he placed Alger Hiss in charge of the Office of Special Political Affairs.

Hiss was to develop and coordinate all policy concerning the United Nations.

This important Kremlin spy and his subversive underlings wrote all the crucial briefs used to guide each facet of U.S. policy!

These papers were used by every American who attended the UN parleys!

The Hiss group also recruited and placed members of the U.S. delegation to the UN!

And they selected all the personnel who served on the staff of the U.S. Representative to the UN!

Alger Hiss was exposed as a Kremlin spy and left the State Department in 1947.

Subversive Dean Rusk took his job as Director of the Office of Special Political Affairs.

Hiss had used his position to place Communist agents in high paying UN jobs!

Dean Rusk continued this treasonous policy, until it was finally brought to light by a Senate Internal Security Subcommittee investigation.

To say the least, many Communists were placed in influential positions at the UN, thanks to subversives like Hiss and Rusk.

Let's take a look at the 17 Americans who were responsible for planning and directing policy leading to the creation of the United Nations!

They were:

William H. Taylor
David Weintraub
Dean Acheson
Victor Perlo
Solomon Adler
Alger Hiss
Laurence Duggan
Harold Glasser
Virginius Frank Coe

Noel Field
Harry Dexter White
Irving Kaplan
William L. Ullman
John Carter Vincent
Abraham George Silverman
Nathan Gregory Silvermaster

With the sole exception of shadowy far-leftist Dean Acheson each of these men was identified as a Soviet espionage agent!

Acheson was never proven to be a Communist spy yet was believed to be one!

His loyal service to the Communist conspiracy began long before the Soviets had even gained diplomatic recognition.

This man was one of two American attorneys employed by Dictator Joseph Stalin, Russia's horrific mass-murderer.

They were selected to represent the interests of his despicable dictatorship in the United States.

Communist espionage agent Alger Hiss was the darling of the Roosevelt's and the Washington *"liberals."*

The other lawyer was Soviet spy Lee Pressman of the Ware cell to which Alger Hiss also belonged!

Pressman was appointed assistant general counsel of the Agricultural Adjustment Administration in 1933 by Secretary of Agriculture Henry A. Wallace.

Shortly thereafter while an official of the Federal government Pressman secretly joined the Communist Party.

Pressman testified that he was active in the Ware group of Communist government employees aiding Soviet intelligence agents.

At least one meeting of the Ware group, he testified, *"Mr. Peter_s may have been present."*

"J. Peters" was a cover name of *NKVD* agent Péter József, the Ware group's control.

Acheson invited Alger's brother Donald who was also a Communist to join his prestigious Washington law firm.

This took place after Donald had been identified as a Russian spy and was forced to leave the State Department!

As could be expected *Time* enthusiastically announced: *"The Secretary-General for the San Francisco Conference was named at Yalta but announced only last week -- lanky Harvard trained Alger Hiss, one of the State Department's brighter young men."*

This was frosting on the Soviet Union's cake! Serving as Secretary-General which was the most powerful position at the UN founding conference was none other than their own man Communist agent Alger Hiss!

The importance of this Kremlin spy cannot be overstressed!

On April 25, 1945, two weeks after President Roosevelt died, Hiss led the U.S. delegation to the UN founding in San Francisco.

Abe Fortas was a Hiss friend from the early thirties when they worked together in the Agricultural Adjustment Administration.

43

He went as an advisor!

The Chicago Tribune reported: *"Fortas helped Alger Hiss and Harry Dexter White, Soviet agents, to draft the United Nations Charter."*

Working closely with Hiss and the other 15 known Kremlin agents at the United Nations Conference on International Organization were over 40 members of the Council on Foreign Relations.

This is an astounding figure in light of the fact that the entire U.S. Delegation numbered less than two hundred!

Dulles was instrumental in getting his close friend Hiss safely out of the State Department when there was imminent danger of his public exposure as a Soviet spy!

These CFR people included such radical leftist luminaries as John Foster Dulles and John J. McCloy.

Dean Acheson and McCloy were instrumental in obtaining diplomatic recognition for Communist Occupied Russia in 1933!

McCloy was the security risk who while Assistant Secretary of War in the Roosevelt Administration approved an order in 1944 allowing Communists to be officers in the U.S. Army!

Also to be found was leftist and CFR stalwart Harold Stassen later to be Eisenhower's traitorous *Battle Act* Administrator.

Stassen's criminal giveaways of strategic goods to America's Red enemies would have made any good Communist agent flush with pride!

Identified Communist Ralph J. Bunche (CFR) was highly visible at the Conference as a top Hiss assistant!

This Red wrote the Charter provision on trusteeship for Hiss.

Extremely serious security risk Philip C. Jessup was another CFR member in attendance!

He'd also been a leading member of the Communist-controlled Institute of Pacific Relations, an organization cited by Congress as being *"considered by the American Communist Party and by Soviet officials as an instrument of Communist policy, propaganda and military intelligence."*

Jessup was later selected by President Eisenhower to serve America's interests as a

justice on the UN World Court.

John Carter Vincent was yet another IPR subversive who was there.

This State Department heavyweight had been identified as a Red espionage agent by former Communist Party official Louis Budenz!

Owen Lattimore (CFR) was a member of the IPR governing board. He was also in attendance!

This security risk was branded by the Senate Internal Security Subcommittee in 1952 as *"a conscious, articulate instrument of the Soviet conspiracy."*

Americans have deliberately been led to believe that the UN was created to be a peace-keeping organization.

This simply isn't so!

Nor was it every intended to be by those who were instrumental in giving it birth!

The passage of time has proven beyond a doubt the not-so-peaceful intent of the UN!

` But prior to this an astute international lawyer had already penned his succinct analysis.

 In August 1945 before the ink on the Charter was even dry Ambassador J. Reuben Clark *(standing on left)* charged: *"There's no provision in the Charter itself that contemplates ending war.*

"The Charter is built to prepare for war, not to promote peace.

"The Charter is a war document not a peace document.

"It doesn't prevent future wars.

"It takes from us the power to declare them, to choose the side on which we shall fight, to determine what forces and military equipment we shall use in the war, and to control and command our sons who do the fighting."

Interestingly enough, Alger Hiss had already worked closely with the Russians in August 1944 as

Executive Secretary of the Dumbarton Oaks Conference in Washington, D.C.

Hiss later became the top State Department advisor to a weak and dying Roosevelt at the Yalta Conference.

Here Hiss and his Communist comrades had agreed on all the important facets of the UN structure and its preposterously deceptive Charter!

Russian-born Leo Pasvolsky (CFR) was called *"the architect of the United Nations Charter."*

Hiss and Pasvolsky worked closely together for a number of years on planning the international organization and drafting the Charter!

Pasvolsky's parents were both active Communists.

This subversive penetrated the government in 1934 and eventually became

49

Chief of the Division of Special Research in the State Department.

One would logically think the UN Charter would be modeled after a time-proven document such as the United States *Constitution*.

It with the *Bill of Rights* guarantees specific freedoms for everyone!

But this was not the case when the United Nations Charter was scripted by the two American Comrades -- Pasvolsky and Hiss!

Rather than bothering to create a document of their own authorship these

Moscow-directed espionage agents simply plagiarized and produced a Charter that was remarkably similar to the Constitution of the Soviet Union!

"The United Nations Charter was written by a State Department-Soviet Union coalition of strategists," charged W. Cleon Skousen, *"who specifically designed the UN so that it could eventually override the sovereign*

independence of its member nations and subject them to the Marxist-dominated World Court and the Marxist-directed military forces of the United Nations.

"Anyone familiar with the Communist Constitution of Russia will recognize in the United Nations Charter a similar format.

"It is characterized by a fervent declaration of democratic principles followed by a limitation which completely nullifies the principles just announced!"

The most shocking aspect of this entire situation is the undisputed fact that Alger Hiss and others were already known to be Communist spies under the direct control of Moscow!

Yet when intelligence reports were sent to their superiors nothing was done to stop them!

Or perhaps because such traitorous activity was openly condoned by the President of the United States nothing could be done!

As an end result, America was duped into joining and financially supporting a subversive organization which was conceived, designed and implemented by men in the employ of Communist Occupied Russia!

There were the Reds in the Kremlin on the one hand!

And on the other were their trusted ideological Comrades secretly planted throughout the United States government!

Leftists of all stripes who push the United Nations today deliberately ignore the crucial roles that spies employed by Moscow played in the founding of the organization!

They conveniently forget to mention the names of Hiss, White, Perlo, Adler, Silverman and other important Reds!

If such names are brought to light, simpering leftist apologists deliberately overlook the fact that these subversives were working for the Soviet Union!

Or they try to play down the importance of such notorious Kremlin espionage agents.

 For example, when President George Bush was Ambassador to the United Nations he parroted the typical apologist malarkey!

Bush unequivocally lied when he said: *"Alger Hiss did not*

work on the Charter draft.

"He served in an administrative post at the San Francisco Conference and was far removed from any policy-forming capacity.

"His duties were of a mechanical nature, such as scheduling of meeting rooms, supplying secretarial help, and similar functions."

Of course Alger Hiss worked on the UN Charter!

He admitted as much when testifying before a 1948 House hearing!

Representative Karl Mundt pointedly asked Hiss about his role.

The Kremlin spy replied: *"I did participate in the creation of the draft that was sent by President Roosevelt to Churchill and Stalin, which was the draft actually adopted at San Francisco."*

Secretary-General Hiss alone was empowered to sign the credentials of every conference delegate allowed in the meeting hall!

Absolutely no one could attend without this man's signature on his I.D. card!

Using this prestigious position Hiss channeled only trusted Comrades into key slots in what was to become the Secretariat!

Yes, Alger Hiss certainly held more than an insignificant "administrative post" as Bush implied!

Time reported: *"Alger Hiss will be an important figure there. As Secretary-General, managing the agenda, he will have a lot to say behind the scenes about who gets the breaks."*

Mr. Hiss most assuredly did!

Clamoring leftist voices still try to hide the traitorous machinations that transpired when the UN was founded.

The United Nations must be a good organization says the propagandists because Stalin was against it from the start!

The Moscow criminals they claim had to be arm-twisted into joining!

Nothing could be further from the truth!

After all why should Communist Occupied Russia shy away from an organization their own people in Moscow and

Washington conceived, created and controlled?

Earl Browder was boss of the Communist Party USA and Stalin's top man in the United States. He said: *"The American Communists worked energetically and tirelessly to lay the foundations for the United Nations, which we were sure would come into existence."*

In fact the Constitution of the Communist Party USA contains a preamble which states: *"The cause of peace and progress require the strengthening of the United Nations as a universal instrument of peace."*

Secretary of State Edward R. Stettinius Jr. (CFR) was in charge of the U.S. delegation to the San Francisco Conference.

Wealthy Hollywood screenwriter Dalton Trumbo was another Hiss selection.

He played an important but little-known role!

The speeches of Stettinius and other conspirators were ghost written by this Red!

Trumbo was one of the infamous Hollywood Ten.

He'd been cited for contempt of Congress during the investigations of Communists in the film industry.
He was identified as a Party member!

Another key figure at the Conference was Treasury's Harry Dexter White (CFR).

This Red espionage agent was there to establish the World Bank which uses American money to play Santa Claus to thankless Communist tyrannies around the globe!

Secretary of State Edward R. Stettinius Jr. (CFR) was in charge of the U.S. delegation to the San Francisco Conference.

Being a part of this United Nation's scam for the United States is like allowing Errol Flynn to take your teenage daughter on an unchaperoned boat ride while you soak up some sun at the beach!

William Ullman was White's chief lieutenant. This subversive was later exposed as a Kremlin spy by former Soviet courier Elizabeth Bentley!

Communists Hiss and White were also the creators of the United Nations Educational, Scientific, and Cultural Organization!

Former Communist Joseph Kornfeder warned: *"UNESCO corresponds to the agitation and propaganda department in the Communist Party."*

For example UNESCO publishes and distributes propaganda world-wide which glorifies life in the Soviet Union!

Such preposterous leftist dross blatantly asserts that Latvia, Estonia, Lithuania and the other Captive Nations voluntarily became a part of Communist Occupied Russia's evil slave labor empire!

Nothing could be further from the truth!

An attempt was made to check on Americans employed in UNESCO.

The SISS reported: *"What appears to be by far the worst danger spot, from the standpoint of disloyalty and subversive activity among Americans is UNESCO.*

"There still exists in UNESCO a clique of people who placed the interests of the Communists and Communist ideology above any service to UNESCO and above their own country.

"Seven employees of UNESCO who were dismissed after refusing to testify before the International Organizations Employees Loyalty Board appealed their dismissals and eventually won decisions awarding them large indemnities, on the ground that the dismissals were improper."

So badly did the Soviet Union want the UN Charter approved by the Senate that they went all out with a fierce propaganda barrage.

The official Party line was `transmitted to American Communists through *Political Affairs:* *"Great popular support and enthusiasm for the United Nations policies should be built up.* *"The opposition must be rendered so impotent that it will be unable to gather any significant support in the Senate against the United Nations Charter and the treaties which will follow."*

The editors of *Life* contributed to the unholy farce!

Their *"Picture of the Week"* featured Soviet agent Alger Hiss as if he were just another loyal American arriving in the nation's Capitol with a large package!

The caption read: *"At the conclusion of the San Francisco Conference the Charter of the United Nations was bundled off to a waiting plane and gingerly placed in a 75-pound fireproof safe equipped with a small parachute.*

"Attached To the safe was a stern inscription: 'Finder -- do not open!

"Notify the Department of State --
Washington, D.C.
"Chief custodian was Conference
Secretary-General Alger Hiss, shown here
with the Charter at the end of the cross-
country trip."

The official Party line was `transmitted
to American Reds through *Political Affairs*.

The Communist stage-managed
acclaim for the UN Charter was eminently
successful.

It was carefully pitched to the powerful
Senate Foreign Relations Committee by

Soviet espionage mole Leo Pasvolsky who was the brazen comrade of Alger Hiss!

Only five days of testimony were required!

The full Senate then shamefully ratified the Charter sight unseen with little debate on July 28, 1945.

The vote was an astounding 89 to 2!

The *Chicago Tribune* described the Charter presentation: *"The hearings in Washington started appropriately enough with a lengthy statement read by Mr. Stettinius but apparently written by Mr. Pasvolsky.*

"When the time came to ask questions Mr. Stettinius gracefully yielded the center of the stage to the same Mr. Pasvolsky who knows all the answers.

"This is more than a little odd. Mr. Pasvolsky's expertise is said to result from the fact that he wrote the original draft of the treaty.

"Nobody has yet explained why the Department entrusted the drafting of this document to a foreign-born functionary."

Dr. Marek Korowicz was a member of Communist Occupied Poland's United

Nations delegation who defected to the United States.

He reminded Americans: *"The Communist Party regards the UN as the most important platform of Soviet propaganda in the world."*

Russian General Bondarenko lectured future Soviet officers at the Frunze Military Academy in Moscow.

His words support those of Korowicz: *"From the rostrum of the United Nations, we shall convince the colonial and semi-colonial people to liberate themselves and to spread the Communist theory over all the world.*

"We recognize the UN as no authority over the Soviet Union, but the United Nations serves to deflect the capitalists and warmongers in the Western world."

Communist Occupied Russia demanded a troika when Swedish Secretary-General Hammarskjold a socialist supporter of world Communism was killed in a 1961 plane crash!

Thant praised Lenin as *"a man with ideals of peace in line with the aims of the UN Charter."*

This was certainly a rather mild description for a despicable mass-murderer!

Thant was assigned two assistants to fulfill the balance of Russia's demands.

One was his trusted KGB Comrade Viktor Mechislavovich Lessiovski from the Soviet Union!

The other was Ralph Bunche who was a protégé of Kremlin, spy Alger Hiss!

This revered and sainted American Comrade was positively identified as a Communist by two former top-ranking American Reds named Leonard Patterson and Manning Johnson!

Yes, the Soviet Union was given their troika!

The neutralist -- a Marxist admirer of Lenin!

The Communist -- a KGB operative from the Soviet Union!

The Westerner – Ralph Bunche who was a Red espionage agent employed by the Kremlin!

But then what else could possibly be expected when the entire hoax was so carefully orchestrated between Washington and Moscow?

Secretariat posts reserved for each country are supposed to be filled by the Secretary General.

Communist Occupied Russia insisted that Moscow select their own nationals!

This guaranteed that the Soviets would have KGB agents in every position open to them.

The presence of U.S. citizens on the staff does little to counter the presence of the KGB!

Various Congressional investigations had shown that a great many Americans working for the UN were also Kremlin spies.

Alger Hiss started it all by initially staffing U.S. positions at the UN with Communist espionage agents.

Subversives running the State Department have since made a habit of obtaining jobs at the UN for government employees in danger of exposure as Red spies.

As a result, America's interests in the UN have been and still are directed by Americans who are subservient to the wishes of Moscow-- not Washington!

During the Korean War a New York Federal Grand Jury uncovered evidence of serious Communist penetration of the American UN staff!

A full-scale inquiry was initiated. Some two hundred American employees to avoid testifying resigned their positions.

Here's the Grand Jury's post-investigation statement: *"Startling evidence has disclosed infiltration into the UN of an overwhelmingly large group of disloyal U.S. citizens, many of whom are closely associated with the international Communist movement.*

"This group numbers scores of individuals, most of whom have long records of federal employment, and at the same time have been connected with persons and organizations subversive to this country."

Due to this investigation and the resulting public clamor the Secretary General who had opposed the investigation was forced to fire a number of American subversives!

But a UN tribunal stacked with Communists and pro-Communists took good care of their own.

They granted $250,000 in cash awards for their Comrades.

Four security risks were actually reinstated with back pay!

Seven others got nice fat payoffs!

Jack Sargent Harris who was a protégé of Communist espionage agent Ralph Bunche pocketed $40,000!

Harris was so serious a security risk that he was denied a clearance and couldn't even get a job with the State Department while Communist spy Alger Hiss reigned supreme!

The publicity generated by the Grand Jury investigation brought on a Senate Judiciary Committee investigation.

Senator James O. Eastland issued this statement: *"There is today in the UN among the American employees there, the greatest concentration of Communists that this Committee has ever encountered.*

"Almost all of these people have, in the past, been employees in the U.S. Government in high and sensitive positions.

"The security officers of our government knew or at least had reason to know that these people have been Communists for many years.

"In fact, some of these people have been the subject of charges before Congress before and during their employment with the UN."

This was further verified by Joseph Kornfeder another Moscow trained American Communist agent who broke with the conspiracy: *"How many Communists, fellow travelers and sympathizers there are among the UN employees, no one seems to know.*

"But judging by their number among the American personnel, there can be no doubt that the Communists control the UN.

"Most of the special agencies at UN headquarters are, in fact, operated by them."

"I realize that the United Nations secretariat cannot recognize Communist affiliations as a bar to employment of persons who are citizens of a Communist state," declared Senator Pat McCarran *"but that is no excuse for allowing one disloyal person to contaminate the American group or misrepresent our ideals."*

The United Nations Charter makes clear provisions for an international militia.

The UN Army is commanded by the Under Secretary-General for Political and Security Council Affairs.

This super-critical post was secretly awarded to the Soviet Union by American traitors at the first UN London Conference in January 1946!

By this agreement only a Russian could hold the position for the initial five years.

Since then no one other than a Communist has been allowed to direct the UN peace keeping forces!

To this day not one American leader has even bothered to request that a non-Communist be given this key job!

Shockingly the USSR has always controlled the UN military arm with the exception of one two year term!

It was then run by a Red from Communist Occupied Yugoslavia who still answered directly to his Kremlin masters!

 If the above sound far-fetched the facts are clearly confirmed by the UN's first Secretary General Trygve Lie who was a fervent socialist from Norway and an idolizer of Stalin!

Even this crypto-Communist was astounded that the United States would agree to such an absurdly dangerous arrangement!

Lie had no idea that Alger Hiss -- the man handling the negotiations on behalf of the United States -- was in the employ of the Soviet international espionage apparatus.

Referring to the first London Conference of 1946, Lie explained: *"Mr. Vyshinsky was the first to inform me of an understanding on the appointment of a Soviet national as Assistant Secretary-General for Political and Security Council Affairs.*

"Mr. Stettinius [U.S. Secretary of State] confirmed to me that he had agreed.

'The preservation of international peace and security was the organization's highest responsibility and it was entrusting the direction of the Secretariat department most concerned with this to a Soviet national that the Americans had agreed."

Such incriminating evidence alone should be reason enough for the United States to abandon the United Nations!

This anti-American organization should be allowed to sink into obscurity under the weight of its bloated Communist bureaucracy!

Simply pull the U.S. out of the UN!

And direct the UN to get out of the U.S.!

This conspiratorial group of anti-American misfits has certainly proven itself unworthy of any further U.S. hospitality.

The United States went to fight the North Korean Reds in what turned out to be no more than a pointless no-win slaughter!

Thanks to the unforgivable machinations of Truman, Americans were forced to go to war under the UN banner.

Here we have a patent absurdity!

General MacArthur was commanding the predominantly American UN forces in battle against the North Korean Communists.

Meanwhile, a Russian Communist thug sitting in the UN was MacArthur's immediate boss!

Communist Occupied Russia's Konstantin E. Zinchenko was directing MacArthur's forces from the UN in New York!

And Communist Occupied China's Mao se Tung was directing the enemy North Korean forces from Peking!

To say the least, many Communists were placed in influential positions at the UN, thanks to subversives like Hiss and Rusk.

So far to the left was Dean Rusk that when he spoke at the University of Pennsylvania in 1951, he compared bloodthirsty Mao Tse-tung to George Washington!

The mass-murdering Chinese Reds were flatteringly described as *"native revolutionaries in the American tradition!"*

As Truman's Assistant Secretary of State for Far Eastern Affairs in 1950 the notorious Dean Rusk was directly responsible for America's treasonous *"no-win"* policy during the Korean War!

This horrendous security risk had a major hand in Truman's firing General MacArthur in 1951, for wanting to go after the retreating Red hordes and win the war!

Dean Rusk, a horrendous security risk had a major hand in Truman's firing of General MacArthur in 1951, for wanting to go after the retreating Red hordes and win the war.

Rusk even had the audacity to write the letter of dismissal for Truman to sign.

Korean troops boldly massacred their American prisoners.

The animalistic Reds forced the men to kneel, tied their hands behind their back with barbed wire and then methodically shot each soldier behind the head with one bullet.

Traitor Rusk was the man behind the disgraceful Korean Armistice where the U.S. agreed in effect to shamefully surrender to the Reds and leave hundreds of American boys behind in POW camps!

A giant piece of America was greatly affected by the Korean War.

33,741 Americans died.

92,134 were wounded.

4,820 were missing in action.

There were 7,245 prisoners of war.

2,847 died in Korean POW camps.

According to our government, 389 POWs were known to have still been alive after all U.S. POWs supposedly returned.

This was a blatant lie and a cover up.

The figure was actually in the thousands.

Not surprisingly both the North Koreans and Red Chinese received top secret military directives from Washington and the United Nations before MacArthur did.

MacArthur's battle plans were always given to the enemy in advance!

Is there any doubt that the United States was deliberately humiliated in the eyes of the world?

Is there any doubt that a no-win war was fought and purposely lost to the militarily inferior North Korean Reds?'

Is there any doubt that the U.S. was made to contemptibly surrender?

Is there any doubt that POWs were shamelessly left behind to rot and die in the prison camps of the North Korean gangsters, Red China and Communist Occupied Russia?

"The public didn't know about those left behind," charged correspondent Carl Rochelle, *"but it is clear that Eisenhower did. Five months after the war, in a document dated December 22, 1953, Secretary of Defense Robert*  *Stevens met with President Eisenhower and told him the Defense Department had the names of 610 Army people and over 300 Air Force prisoners still held by the North Koreans."*

What did the United Nations do about this?

Absolutely nothing!

Retired Colonel Phillip Corso was an aide to Eisenhower. He observed the exchange of prisoners at Panmunjon and was able to speak with some of those who came back: *"Our own boys told me there were sick and wounded American boys not 10 miles from the camp, and they were not exchanged."*

What did the United Nations do?

Absolutely nothing!

A former Czechoslovakian general and Soviet intelligence agent Jan Sejna defected to the United States before the end of the Cold War.

He told Congress that he saw some of the prisoners being used in gruesome medical experiments: *"The top-secret purpose of the hospital was medical experimentation on Americans and South Koreans.*

"The POWs were used to test the effects of chemical and biological weapons, and test the effects of atomic radiation.

"The Soviets also used the American prisoners to test the psychological endurance of American soldiers. They were also used to test various mind controls."

What did the United Nations do about this?

Absolutely nothing!

Air Force General George Stratemeyer said this regarding one of the lessons learned by the United States after being defeated in the Korean War: *"Don't ever fight under the United Nations.*

"You will not be permitted to win!"

And indeed there are other examples as well.

The United Nations eagerly almost blithely orchestrated the *"peacekeeping"* charade in the Congo, during the early Sixties!

The UN action consisted of the savage butchery of unarmed men, women the elderly and children!

An incredible orgy of mass-murder, rape and cannibalism was carried out with the UN's blessing!

The mayhem was directed by savage animalistic Congolese troops against rebelling forces led by Katanga's President Moise Tshombe.

Tshombe had three strikes against him when he tried to secede Katanga from the chaotic Central Congolese Communist dictatorship.

He was anti-Communist!

He was pro-American!

And he was a professed Christian!

These were all negative attributes from the standpoint of the atheistic immoral madmen who run the United Nations!

Harlan Cleveland was a major force behind pushing the UN war against Tshombe!

Crazed Congolese troops high on hashish and thirsting for blood were heavily armed and transported to Katanga in American supplied transport planes!

Red Cross markings on hospital walls and roofs were used as targets for mortaring, bombing and strafing practice!

These maniacs used bazookas to blow up clearly marked ambulances enroute to and from hospitals!

UN mercenaries forced their way into hospitals in Elizabethville and sadistically machine-gunned and macheted helpless bed-ridden patients!

Telegrams of protest were sent by 46 doctors in Elizabethville to Pope John Paul, President Kennedy and 14 other world leaders.

Small children, babies and the elderly were wantonly bayoneted by the unbridled savages!

Atrocities committed against the civilian population were extensive!

They implored them to stop the terrorist bombardment of hospitals and civilian populations.

Nothing was done!

The Catholic bishop in Elizabethville told how terrorist UN soldiers deliberately murdered innocent men, women and children and looted and destroyed churches!

Nothing was done to put an end to the terrible punishment the UN was inflicting in the name of *"peacekeeping."*

Tshombe was later a captive in Communist Occupied Algeria and was horribly tortured and subsequently executed!

No one at the UN ever mentions the naked terrorist aggressions including rapes and murder witnessed in the Communist takeovers of Cuba, Rhodesia, Nicaragua, and other countries!

It should come as no surprise that the UN never takes action against Communist acts of terrorism.

Communist Occupied Russia made a heinous practice of dropping plane loads of harmless appearing harmonicas, radios, toy trucks, plastic pens and colorful birds in Afghanistan.

These booby-traps would explode when picked up or accidentally stepped on by children!

The Soviet toy-bombs were designed to blind kids and blow their hands or feet off rather than kill them!

The Russians saw this as an efficient and quite practical method of both terrorizing and demoralizing the people of Afghanistan.

And they were also eliminating a future generation of anti-Communist Afghan Freedom Fighters!

What did the UN do?

The UN did nothing!

What did the UN say?

The UN said nothing!

In another instance, the UN even refused to pass a resolution condemning Communist Occupied China for its atrocious rape of Tibet!

And nothing was done by he United Nations to stop the Communist Khmer Rouge's genocidal spree in which they murdered more than one-third of the Cambodian people!

But the Cambodian super criminal Communist leaders did get a standing ovation at the UN for their deadly handiwork!

An article in the *Santa Ana Register* noted: *"Most folks like the United Nations on the grounds that the UN is a 'peacemaking' organization.*

"Now, that simply isn't so.

"The method of the UN is to use armed might against any nation presumed to be an aggressor [with the exception of Communist dictatorships].

"Its function is to make war.

"Though it professes peace, it is obviously a war-making agency."

The United Nations is far from mankind's last and only hope for world peace!

Yet it is the perfect organization to bring about *"world peace"* by the Communist definition -- the absence of opposition to Communism!

It is not the only vehicle around necessary to prevent a nuclear holocaust!

In fact just the opposite is the case!

The UN isn't the epitome of man's unselfish aspirations!

It isn't man's greatest triumph!

Instead it's really no more than a monument to the greed of evil men.

The UN was brought about to foster traitorous unilateral disarmament in the United States!

All American weapons including nuclear are eventually to be turned over to a Red controlled international *"peacekeeping"* Army.

The UN was created to redistribute America's great wealth!

The Marxist schemers plan to ultimately take from those who have and give it to the international have-nots no matter how undeserving those have-nots may be!

The UN was formulated as a means to negate the U.S. Constitution and end American sovereignty!

To do away with nationhood!

It was from the very beginning to be the vehicle for eventually attaining a world dictatorship!

The dream of the Communist schemers in the UN is to manage a global government from Moscow.

The dream of the socialist schemers in the UN meshes with that of their Communist brothers!

They claim to disagree only with the methods used *(mass murder, terrorism, etc.)* in achieving the desired end result.

But even this difference is questionable!

Milton Eisenhower couldn't have made it any clearer in reference to the UN: *"We should view our latest attempt to create a true world government.*

"Every member is committed to the sacrifice of individual sovereignty . . . commitment to limited sovereignty marks . . .

a considerable advance in our progress toward world government."

The late Gary Allen charged: *"Never before in recorded history has a nation permitted an avowed enemy openly to pursue its policies of conquest on its home territory within so vast a diplomatic sanctuary -- a sanctuary supposedly dedicated to peace.*

"At least Steuben should be employed to

remodel the glass palace on the East River in the shape of a Trojan Horse."

Scott Stanley, Jr. quite correctly declared: *"For the greatest nation on earth to sit down in a Byzantine parliament of man with mass murderers and dope pushers and assassins and terrorists and torturers and pathetic creatures in loin cloths is as ludicrous on its face as the United Nations is sinister in its purpose."*

Equatorial Guinea's national anthem *is "Let's Walk Through the Jungle of Our Immense Happiness!"*

Tanzania citizens are flogged for wearing tight clothing!

Somalia executes men before a firing squad for "undermining the government's authority" by opposing a law giving equal rights to women!

Edward Mukuka Nkoloso trained 12 Zambian astronauts including a 16-year-old girl friend by spinning them around a tree in an oil drum and teaching them to walk on their hands because he explained that this is *"the only way humans can walk on the moon."*

He's a grade-school science teacher and the director of Zambia's National Academy of Science, Space Research and Philosophy.

This character had the nerve to apply for a $19.6 million loan for his space program saying *"We are delaying our plans to plant the Zambian flag on the moon.*

"My spacemen (they wear red and green Superman capes) demanded payment and refused to continue with our program of rolling down hills in oil drums and my special tree-swinging methods of simulating space weightlessness."

Gabon's first President Leon M'ba did time in a French prison for cannibalism and for selling human meat!

President for Life of the Central African Republic got into a controversy over his choice of cannibalistic bedtime snacks!

Samora Machel of Mozambique practiced cannibalism when he ate human flesh during his many Satanic Voodoo ceremonies!

Mozambique's later President Joaquim Chissano was commonly known to eat human flesh during witchcraft rituals!

And lastly and almost laughable is Zaire's President for Life Mobutu Sese Seko Kuku-Ngbendu Wa-Za-Banga. Interpretation: *"Mobutu the peppery, all-conquering warrior, the cock who leaves no hen intact!"*

Epilogue

The record covering crucial episodes of the McCarthy era has been massively and deliberately distorted from the very beginning!

Conveniently forgotten or deliberately overlooked are the 78 hearings held between 1951 and 1952 by Senator William E. Jenner's (R-Indiana) Senate Internal Security Subcommittee (SISS); the House Committee On Internal Security; the House Un-American Activities Committee (HUAC) under the chairmanship of both Martin Dies (D-Texas) and Francis Walters (D-Pa); the Federal Bureau of Investigation (FBI) under the guidance of J. Edgar Hoover; and other investigating committees and individuals.

Out of all of these investigations one man was selected:

To be stopped!

To be destroyed!

To be made an example!

Why?

So that no one would ever again dare to initiate any investigations into the penetration of our government agencies by communist agents (spies) in the employ of the Soviet Union!

Yes!

An obscure Senator from Wisconsin was deliberately targeted for this purpose!

Joseph McCarthy's incredibly successful investigations panicked those on the political left.

Their reaction was shockingly quick!

Key data was been suppressed, denied and even widely falsified.

This took place in the media, all branches of government and many alleged scholars entrenched in the ivory towers of our institutions of higher learning!

Such misreporting and misrepresentation of the facts continues today.

Much of the misinformation we were (and still are today) so carefully spoon-fed about Senator Joseph McCarthy the man and his investigations was no more than an admixture of uncheckable blovations from deceased third parties and demonstratable falsehoods!

For example, how many innocent people were harmed by McCarthy's revelations?

The correct answer?

Not one!

No!

Not One!

McCarthy's most virulent critics have had more than a half century to produce the names of the hundreds of innocent people they claim were destroyed by the astounding revelations of the Senator from Wisconsin.

Yet those highly skilled propagandists in our media and government and institutions of higher learning have been unable to name even one innocent person they claim was destroyed after being falsely accused by McCarthy!

How many innocent people committed suicide as a result of McCarthy's exposure?

The correct answer?

Not one!

Not one suicide can be attributed to the investigations conducted by McCarthy!

No! Not one!

According to the obscene claims made the highly skilled propagandists in our media, government and scholars entranced in those ivory towers of our colleges and universities there were a   rash of suicides with bodies falling constantly of the heads of pedestrians below on the streets of Manhattan!

Once again, McCarthy's most virulent critics have had more than 50 years to produce the names of the hundreds of innocent people they claim committed suicide because of the astounding revelations of the Senator from Wisconsin.

Yet those highly skilled propagandists in our media and government and institutions of higher learning have been unable to name even one innocent person they claim committed suicide after being falsely accused by McCarthy!

No!

Not one!

But there were two suicides on record during the McCarthy period!

Neither was the result of an innocent person who'd been ruined by McCarthy's revelations!

Both were subversives who'd been exposed by McCarthy!

Both were subversives who'd been positively indentified as Kremlin agents!

Lawrence Duggan had been operating in the State Department as a widely known Soviet spy!

He'd been called to testify before a Congressional investigating committee.

Duggan never made it!

He conveniently "fell" from a window high up in a Manhattan skyscraper!

Fell?

Probably not!

He was more than likely pushed from or tossed out of the window by an assassin in the employ of the Soviet Union!

Why?

To make certain he didn't fold under pressure and start naming other Kremlin moles.

Secondly there was the unexpected demise of Harry Dexter White.

This Soviet agent discovered that he was being investigated by J. Edgar Hoover of the FBI!

He died of a sudden heart attack!

Coincidence?

Not hardly!

Was White's death a suicide?

Yes or at least so claimed McCarthy's critics!

Again, not hardly!

Heart attacks can readily be induced with the proper use of certain medicines administered by a hired assassin in the employ of the Kremlin!

Why?

Simply to eliminate anyone who might panic and decide to turncoat and reveal the names of other spies secretly entrenched deeply in the bowels of every branch of our government.

To sum up, most fit into one of three categories:

Conscience lacking incurable liars!

Those with an axe to grind!

Individuals who simply do not know the facts!

If you liked this book in the *None Dare Call It Treason* series then you'll probably also enjoy reading the others!

Gift copies of this book can be ordered at robertwpelton.com

Available Titles

None Dare Call It Treason Book 1
The Internal Security Farce!
5.5" x 8.5" 103 pages $4.95
Order from **robertwpelton.com**

None Dare Call It Treason Book 2
Never Ending Subversion In Government!
5.5" x 8.5" 99 pages $4.95
Order from **robertwpelton.com**

None Dare Call It Treason Book 3
*America's Subversive State Department
Bloated With Security Risks*
5.5" x 8.5" 98 pages $4.95
Order from **robertwpelton.com**

None Dare Call It Treason Book 4
*America's Illustrious State Department!
It's Machiavellian Misdeeds!*
5.5" x 8.5" 106 pages $4.95
Order from **robertwpelton.com**

None Dare Call It Treason Book 5
Our Presidents A Major Security Threat!
5.5" x 8.5" 73 pages $4.95
Order from **robertwpelton.com**

None Dare Call It Treason Book 6
Presidential Words & Deeds
&Blatant Lies!
5.5" x 8.5" 128 pages $4.95
Order from **robertwpelton.com**

None Dare Call It Treason Book 7
Subversives Close To Our Presidents
5.5" x 8.5" 104 pages $4.95
Order from **robertwpelton.com**

None Dare Call It Treason Book 8
Henry Kissinger
The Shadowy Untouchable Kremlin Spy!
5.5" x 8.5" 74 pages $4.95
Order from **robertwpelton.com**

None Dare Call It Treason Book 9
Inexcusably Arming America's Enemies!
5.5" x 8.5" 102 pages $4.95
Order from **robertwpelton.com**

None Dare Call It Treason Book 10
*Inexcusably Financing
America's Enemies!*
5.5" x 8.5" 102 pages $4.95
Order from **robertwpelton.com**

None Dare Call It Treason Book 11
*Treasonous   Trade With & Aid To
Enemies Of Freedom!*
5.5" x 8.5" 93 pages $4.95
Order from **robertwpelton.com**

None Dare Call It Treason Book 12
*Wholesale Treason During the War
In Vietnam!*
5.5" x 8.5" 120 pages $4.95
Order from **robertwpelton.com**

None Dare Call It Treason Book 13
*Big Business
& Astounding Acts Of Treason!*
5.5" x 8.5" 93 pages $4.95
Order from **robertwpelton.com**

None Dare Call It Treason Book 14
*Illegally Importing
Slave Made Goodies!*

5.5" x 8.5" 91 pages $4.95
Order from **robertwpelton.com**

None Dare Call It Treason Book 15

The House That Hiss Built
The Anti-American United Nations!
5.5" x 8.5" 117 pages $4.95
Order from **robertwpelton.com**

None Dare Call It Treason Book 16

Security Risks in the House and Senate!
5.5" x 8.5" 62 pages $4.95
Order from **robertwpelton.com**

None Dare Call It Treason Book 17

The Supreme Court A Devastating
Threat To National Security!
5.5" x 8.5" 90 pages $4.95
Order from **robertwpelton.com**

Orders for Resale
40% Off Retail Price

Send Purchase Order to

christianamerica2@yahoo.com

MEET THE
AUTHOR

Robert W. Pelton has been writing for more than 45 years on political and historical subjects.

He has published more than 100 books including the sensational *Unwanted Dead or Alive – The Greatest Act of Treason in Our History*

Mr. Pelton proudly claims a heritage going all the way back to well before the War for American Independence.

One of his ancestors, John Rogers, came to America on the Mayflower and was one of 41 signers of the Mayflower Compact.

Another, John Smith was one of the founders of Jamestown.

Peleg Pelton served as the fifer in the Continental Army at age 17 during the Battle of Saratoga (1777) and again in Yorktown (1781).

Captain Peter Hager was Commander of the Old Stone Fort in Schoharie, New York, in 1780.

Mr. Pelton is a member of Sons of the Revolution (SOR), and Sons of the American Revolution (SAR).

www.ingramcontent.com/pod-product-compliance
Lightning Source LLC
Chambersburg PA
CBHW070358290526
45790CB00004B/1550